ESSENTIA

MICROWAVE RECIPES

TARLA DALAL

S&C

Price Rs. 189/-

Published & Distributed by : **Sanjay & Company**

353/A-1, Shah & Nahar Industrial Estate, Dhanraj Mill Compound,
Lower Parel (W), Mumbai - 400 013. INDIA.
Tel. : (91-22) 2496 8068 • Fax : (91-22) 2496 5876 • E-mail : sanjay@tarladalal.com

Printed by : **Jupiter Prints**, Mumbai

OTHER BOOKS BY TARLA DALAL

INDIAN COOKING
Tava Cooking
Rotis & Subzis
Desi Khana
The Complete Gujarati Cook Book
Mithai
Chaat
Achaar aur Parathe
The Rajasthani Cookbook
Swadisht Subzian

TOTAL HEALTH
Low Calorie Healthy Cooking
Pregnancy Cookbook
Baby and Toddler Cookbook
Cooking with 1 Teaspoon of Oil
Home Remedies
Delicious Diabetic Recipes
Fast Foods Made Healthy
Healthy Soups & Salads
Healthy Breakfast
Calcium Rich Recipes New
Healthy Heart Cook Book New
Forever Young Diet New
Healthy Snacks New

WESTERN COOKING
The Complete Italian Cookbook
The Chocolate Cookbook
Eggless Desserts
Mocktails & Snacks
Soups & Salads
Mexican Cooking
Easy Gourmet Cooking
Chinese Cooking
Easy Chinese Cooking
Thai Cooking
Sizzlers & Barbeques

MINI SERIES
A new world of Idlis & Dosas
Cooking under 10 minutes
Pizzas and Pastas
Fun Food for Kids
Roz Ka Khana
Microwave - Desi Khana
T.V. Meals
Paneer
Parathas
Chawal
Dals
Sandwiches

GENERAL COOKING
Exciting Vegetarian Cooking
Quick & Easy Cooking
Saatvik Khana
Mixer Cook Book
The Pleasures of Vegetarian Cooking
The Delights of Vegetarian Cooking
The Joys of Vegetarian Cooking

Cooking With Kids
Snacks Under 10 Minutes
Ice-Cream & Frozen Desserts
Desserts Under 10 Minutes
Entertaining
Microwave Snacks & Desserts New

Contents

G. Desserts

H. Sweets

While every effort has been taken to ensure that the cooking time is accurate each time you try a recipe, this may not happen always.

The timing may change slightly. And for a host of reasons. Reasons that you and we cannot really control. Like voltage fluctuations, changes in the quantity, the inherent water / fat / sugar content of different foods, the starting temperatures and so on.

All these affect the cooking times in different ways.

For instance, when cooking quantities more than those specified in the recipes, the timing does not increase in exact proportion to the increase in the food quantity. So, when the quantity is doubled, the time increase is only 40-45% and not 100% Similarly, when you use more than necessary water, cooking will take longer.

Please do bear these things in mind and set your own judgements on timings. This way you will get a better idea on how they do change, even if they do not change very much.

General Microwave Tips:

★ For best cooking results, use heat resistant glass, ceramic, china or porcelain dishes.

★ For low heat cooking such as reheating or for very short heating times, strong plastic containers will also do.

★ Small, uniformly shaped, pieces or amounts of food will cook quicker than large ones.

★ Stirring or rearranging food once or twice during cooking helps it cook more evenly.

★ Never hesitate to open the door midway through cooking to see the food or to stir it.

★ If you open the door midway to stir or rearrange, remember to press the START switch once again after closing the door, to continue cooking.

★ Standing time is an integral part of most cooking. Therefore, some foods that do not seem completely cooked when removed from the microwave, will get cooked during standing time.

★ To blanch badaam, boil one cup of water, add the nuts and microwave again for about 30 seconds on level H. The skin slips off easily.

★ Warm a lemon (or any citrus fruit) for about 25 to 40 second on level High.
Allow the fruit to stand for a minute before squeezing it. This makes the fruit yield more juice.

★ To reheat bread or chappatis without drying them out, wrap them in paper towels for better results.

★ To get rid of food odour from the cooker, put a piece of lime in a cup of water and microwave for about 60 seconds on level H.

★ To defrost frozen vegetable, pierce the bag or loosen the container slightly. Defrosting normally takes 4 to 6 minutes.

★ Do not deep or shallow fry in the microwave. The oil temperature cannot be controlled.

★ Do not boil eggs in the cooker. They will explode.

★ You can warm baby's milk straight in the feeding bottle. 15 seconds to 45 seconds will make it just right or warm, depending on how hot your baby likes it.

★ When cooking or reheating two dishes together, remember that different foods require different cooking or reheating times. Therefore, remove the dish that cooks faster as soon as it is done or it will overcook.

★ Do not be afraid to look into the cooker through the door.

★ When removing a dish from the cooker, first check the container's temperature by touching it. Normally the dish does not get hot but the food inside, can and does, pass on heat to the container by conduction. If it is hot, use mittens.

★ After serving yourself, if you find that the food has gone cold, you can put your dinner plate into the cooker for reheating. Heat on level H for 1½ – 2 minutes, depending on how hot you like your food.

INTRODUCTION

Vegetarian cooking on the microwave is very fast, very healthy and very easy. Microwaving gives you food with practically all nutrients intact, with a minimum of fuss and effort. And in next to no time at all.

Microwaves work on a very simple principle. Of creating heat by friction. Being a form of radiowaves, microwaves vibrate at very high speeds and agitate the water molecules present in all primary foods. And when these molecules of water rub against each other, they create friction, which in turn produces heat. This heat, then, cooks the food.

What's more this heat is generated from the water in the food. Which leads to a substantial reduction in cooking time, unlike conventional cooking where first the utensil gets heated, which in turn passes the heat onto the food, which then cooks.

What follows automatically after this reduction in cooking time, is enhanced nutrition value. With microwaving, then, most of the nutrients remain in the food and don't escape.

To all these advantages of microwaving, add Mrs. Tarla Dalal's ingenuity in using microwaves so effectively for Indian vegetarian cooking. Proving conclusively, once and for all, that an appliance which was indispensable and unmatched for its reheating capabilities, has the power to do so much more.

The following pages will lead you through over 50 recipes. Categorized into sections for easy reference, these recipes are just the beginning. And will serve their full purpose when they have managed to show you how you can really let your imagination do wonders.

Basic Recipes

Cheese Sauce

Pouring Consistency ● Cooking time : 0 mins. 50 secs. ● Makes 1 teacup

1 tbsp butter
1 tbsp plain flour (maida)
2 tbsp grated cheese
1 teacup milk
salt and pepper to taste

1. Put the butter in a glass bowl and microwave on HIGH for about 10 seconds.
2. Add the flour and microwave on HIGH for 20 seconds, stirring once in-between after 10 seconds.
3. Add the milk and cheese and microwave on HIGH for about 20 seconds. Do not boil.
4. Add salt and pepper.

* Use as required.

Tomato Sauce

Pouring Consistency ● **Cooking time : 9 mins. 45 secs.** ● **Makes 1 teacup**

3 medium red tomatoes
1/2 onion, chopped
2 cloves garlic, crushed
1/2 tsp chilli powder
2 tbsp tomato ketchup
1 tsp cornflour, mixed with 5 tbsp water
1 tsp sugar
1 tbsp butter
salt to taste

1. Cut the tomatoes into big pieces. Put them into a shallow dish and microwave on HIGH for 4 to 5 minutes. Blend in a liquidiser and strain.

2. Put the butter in a glass bowl and melt it by microwaving on HIGH for about 15 seconds.

3. Add the onion and garlic and SIMMER (Cook Level 5) for about 1½ minutes.

4. Add the tomato puree, chilli powder, tomato ketchup, cornflour mixture, sugar and salt. Microwave on HIGH for 3 minutes, stirring in-between after every 1 minute.

* Use as required.

Boiled Pasta

Cooking time : 7 mins. 30 secs.

Serves 4

250 grams pasta (noodles/spaghetti/ macaroni)
1 tsp oil
salt to taste

1. Put 1 1/2 litres of water in a glass bowl. Microwave on HIGH for 2½ minutes and bring to a boil.
2. Add the oil, pasta and salt and microwave on HIGH for about 4 to 5 minutes, stirring once in-between after 2 minutes.
3. Remove from the cooker, cover and allow to stand for 1 to 2 minutes in case of noodles (3 to 4 minutes in case of spaghetti and macaroni). Drain.

* Use as required.

White Sauce

Pouring Consistency ● Cooking time : 0 mins. 50 secs. ● Makes 1 teacup

1 tbsp butter
1 tbsp plain flour (maida)
1 teacup milk
salt and pepper to taste

1. Put the butter in a glass bowl and microwave on HIGH for about 10 seconds.
2. Add the flour and microwave on HIGH for 20 seconds, stirring once in-between after 10 seconds.
3. Add the milk and microwave on HIGH for about 20 seconds. Do not boil.
4. Add salt and pepper.

* Use as required.

Soups

Spinach Soup

PICTURE ON PAGE 17

Cooking time : 5 mins. 45 secs.   Serves 2

2 teacups spinach leaves
1 tbsp butter
1 tbsp plain flour (maida)
1/2 teacup milk
salt and pepper to taste

1. Thoroughly wash the spinach and remove the thick stems.
2. Put the spinach leaves in a plate and microwave on HIGH for about 30 seconds, until the spinach is well cooked.
3. Blend the spinach to a smooth puree in a blender.
4. Put the butter in a glass bowl and microwave on HIGH for 15 seconds.
5. Add the flour and microwave on HIGH for 1 minute or until the surface looks puffy.
6. Add the milk, spinach puree, salt and pepper. Microwave on HIGH for 4 minutes, stirring once in-between after 2 minutes.

* Serve hot.

Golden Broth

Cooking time : 11 mins.   Serves 2

1 large carrot, sliced
1 large potato, sliced
2 tbsp chopped onion
1/2 teacup milk
1 tbsp butter
salt and pepper to taste

1. Sprinkle 3 to 4 tablespoons of water over the carrot and potato and microwave on HIGH for 7 minutes.
2. Add 1 1/2 teacups of water and blend in a liquidiser. Strain.
3. Put the butter in a glass bowl and microwave on HIGH for 1 minute, stirring once in-between after 30 seconds.
4. Add the prepared puree, onion milk, salt and pepper. Microwave on HIGH for about 3 minutes, stirring in-between after every 1 minute.

* Serve hot.

Quick Corn Soup

Cooking time :   6 mins. 15 secs.   Serves 4

3/4 teacup canned corn or frozen,
precooked, tender corn
1 onion, finely chopped
3 teacups milk
1 1/2 tbsp plain flour (maida)
1 tbsp butter
salt and pepper to taste

1. Mix the milk, 3 teacups of water and the flour.
2. Put the butter in a glass bowl and microwave on HIGH for about 15 seconds. Add the onion and microwave on HIGH for 1 minute, stirring once in-between after 30 seconds.
3. Add the flour mixture and the corn and microwave on HIGH for about 4 to 5 minutes, stirring in-between after every 1 minute. While stirring, check each time that the soup does not stick to the bottom of the vessel.
4. Add salt and pepper.

* Serve hot.

Potage Darblay

Cooking time : 14 mins. 35 secs.

For the soup

450 grams potatoes
225 grams onions
2 teacups milk
2 tbsp butter
1 bay leaf
4 tbsp fresh cream
salt and pepper to taste

For the topping

1 carrot
1 onion
4 fresh beans
1 tbsp butter

For the soup

1. Slice the potatoes and onions thinly.
2. Put 1 tbsp butter in a glass bowl and microwave on HIGH for 20 seconds.
3. Add the potatoes and onions and microwave on HIGH for 2 to 3 minutes.
4. Add the milk, 3 teacups of water and the bay leaf. Microwave on HIGH for 5 to 6 minutes, stirring once in-between after 3 minutes. Thereafter, take out the bay leaf.
5. Blend the mixture in a liquidiser.
6. Microwave on HIGH for about 2 to 3 minutes.

For the topping

1. Cut the vegetables for the topping like match sticks.
2. Put the butter in a glass bowl and microwave in HIGH for about 15 seconds.
3. Add the vegetables and 1/2 teacup of water. Microwave on HIGH for about 2 minutes.

How to serve

Just before serving, add the boiled vegetables for the topping, the cream, salt and pepper to the soup.

* Serve hot.

Cream of Lettuce Soup

Cooking time : 4 mins. 50 secs.   Serves 6

2 teacups chopped lettuce leaves
2 onions
3 teacups milk
2 tbsp plain flour (maida)
2 tbsp butter
salt and pepper to taste

1. Chop the lettuce and onion.
2. Put the lettuce leaves in a bowl and microwave on HIGH for about 30 seconds.
3. Put the butter in a glass bowl and microwave on HIGH for 20 seconds. Add the onions and microwave on HIGH for 1 minute . or until light pink in colour.
4. Blend the lettuce and onions to a smooth puree in a blender. Strain.
5. Mix the milk, plain flour and add to the puree. Add 3 teacups of water.
6. Cover and microwave on HIGH for about 3 minutes, stirring once in-between after 1 1/2 minutes.
7. Add salt and pepper.

* Serve hot.

Mushroom Soup

Cooking time : 8 mins. 15 secs.   **Serves 4**

200 grams fresh button mushrooms
1 onion, chopped
2 tsp butter
salt and pepper to taste

1. Chop the mushrooms.
2. Put the butter in a glass bowl and microwave on HIGH for 15 seconds. Add the onion and microwave on HIGH for 1 1/2 minutes or until light pink in colour, stirring once in-between after 45 seconds.
3. Add the mushrooms and 4 teacups of water, cover and microwave on HIGH for about 6 to 6 1/2 minutes.
4. When cooked, blend in a liquidiser.
5. Add salt and pepper.

* Serve hot.

Milk Vegetable Soup

Cooking time : 7 mins. 20 secs.

Serves 6

2 teacups finely chopped mixed
vegetables
(french beans, carrots, green peas)
1 onion, chopped
2 tbsp butter
1 1/2 tbsp plain flour (maida)
4 teacups milk
salt and pepper to taste

1. Place the vegetables in a shallow
   dish. Sprinkle 5 to 6 tablespoons
   of water on top and microwave on
   HIGH for about 3 to 4 minutes.
2. Put the butter in a glass bowl and
   microwave on HIGH for 20
   seconds. Add the onion and
   microwave on HIGH for about 1
   minute, stirring once in-between
   after 30 seconds.
3. Add the vegetables and 1 teacup of
   water.
4. Mix the flour and milk and add to
   the vegetables. Microwave on
   HIGH for 1 1/2 to 2 minutes.
5. Add salt and pepper.

* Serve hot.

SPINACH SOUP
For recipe see page 10

Vegetables

Paneer Methi Palak

Cooking time : 7 mins. 25 secs.   Serves 2

3 teacups chopped spinach
3/4 teacup fresh fenugreek (methi)
leaves
1 onion chopped
15 mm piece ginger, finely chopped
2 1/2 green chillies, finely chopped
75 grams sliced paneer
1/2 tsp amchur powder
3 tsp oil
salt to taste

1. Thoroughly wash the spinach and fenugreek and remove the thick stems.
2. Put them in a plate and microwave on HIGH for about 40 seconds.
3. Blend the cooked leaves to a smooth puree in a blender.
4. Put the oil in a glass bowl and microwave on HIGH for 30 seconds.
5. Add the onion and microwave on HIGH for 2 minutes or until light pink in colour.
6. Add the ginger and green chillies and microwave on HIGH for 15 seconds.
7. Add the puree, paneer, amchur powder and salt. Cover and microwave on HIGH for 3 to 4 minutes.

* Serve hot.

STUFFED LADIES FINGERS
For recipe see page 20

Stuffed Ladies Fingers

PICTURE ON PAGE : 18

Cooking time : 5 mins.   Serves 2

200 grams ladies fingers(bhendi)
1/4 grated fresh coconut
2 1/2 tbsp chopped coriander
2 tbsp coriander-cumin seed
(dhana-jira)powder
2 tsp sugar
1 tsp red chilli powder
a pinch of asafoetida
1 tbsp oil
salt to taste

1. Make slits on the ladies fingers.
2. Mix all the other ingredients very well and stuff into the ladies fingers.
3. Arrange in a shallow glass dish and sprinkle a little oil and 1 tablespoon of water. Microwave on HIGH for about 4 to 5 minutes.

* Serve hot.

Stuffed Potatoes

Cooking time : 12 mins.   Serves 2

200 grams small potatoes with jackets.
1/4 grated fresh coconut
2 1/2 tbsp chopped coriander
2 tsp coriander-cumin seed
(dhana-jira) powder
2 tsp sugar
1 tsp red chilli powder
a pinch of asafoetida
salt to taste

1. Wash the potatoes. Make slits on them. If you want, remove the skin.
2. Bake the potatoes on HIGH for about 6 to 7 minutes.
3 .Mix all the other ingredients very well and stuff into the potatoes.
4. Arrange in a shallow dish and sprinkle a little oil and 1 1/2 tablespoons of water. Microwave on HIGH for 4 to 5 minutes.

* Serve hot.

Vegetable Makhanwala

Cooking time : 9 mins. 45 secs. Serves 4

50 grams french beans cut diagonally
50 grams cauliflower, cut into strips
or cubes
50 grams carrots, cut into long strips
or cubes
1/2 teacup green peas
1 onion sliced
1/2 teacup fresh cream
1 tbsp plain flour (maida)
1/2 teacup milk
2 tbsp tomato ketchup
1 tbsp butter
1/4 tsp chilli powder
salt to taste

1. Put the french beans, cauliflower, carrots and peas in a shallow dish, sprinkle 5 to 6 tablespoons of water and microwave on HIGH for about 5 minutes.
2. Put the butter in a glass bowl and microwave on HIGH for about 15 seconds. Add the onions and microwave on HIGH for 1¹/₂ minutes or until light pink in colour.
3. Mix the cream, flour, milk and tomato ketchup and add to the onions. Add the vegetables, chilli powder and salt and microwave on HIGH for 3 minutes.

* Serve hot.

Masala Vegetable

Cooking time : 10 mins.   Serves 2

50 grams brinjals
50 grams potatoes
50 grams green peas
1 onion, chopped
2 tbsp chopped coriander
1/4 tsp turmeric powder
2 tsp coriander-cumin seed
(dhana-jira) powder
2 tsp chilli powder
1/2 tsp garam masala
2 tbsp oil
salt to taste
1 tbsp chopped coriander for
decoration

To be ground into a paste

2 tbsp grated fresh coconut
2 green chillies
12 mm piece ginger
5 to 6 cloves garlic

1. Cut the vegetables into big pieces
2. Mix the chopped onion, coriander, turmeric powder, coriander- cumin seed powder, chilli powder, garam masala, oil, paste, salt and 1 teacup of water. Add the vegetable and green peas
3. Cover and microwave on HIGH for 10 minutes, stirring twice in-between after every 3 minutes.

* Serve hot. Decorate with coriander

Vegetables in Creamy Sauce

Cooking time : 11 mins. 45 secs.   **Serves 2**

50 grams french beans
50 grams carrots
50 grams green peas
1 onion, finely chopped
1 tomato, finely chopped
1/2 teacup fresh cream
1 tbsp plain flour (maida)
1/2 teacup milk
2 tbsp tomato ketchup
1 tbsp butter
1/4 tsp chilli powder
salt to taste

1. Cut the french beans and carrots into long strips.
2. Put the french beans, carrots and green peas in a shallow dish, sprinkle 5 to 6 tablespoons of water and microwave on HIGH for about 5 to 6 minutes.
3. Mix the cream, flour, milk and tomato ketchup.
4. Put the butter in a glass bowl and microwave on HIGH for about 15 seconds.
5. Add the onion and microwave on HIGH for 1 minute 30 seconds or till light pink in colour.
6. Add the tomato, vegetables, prepared sauce, chilli powder and salt and microwave on HIGH for 4 minutes, stirring once in-between after 2 minutes.

* Serve hot.

Variation : Corn and Peas in Creamy Sauce.
Use 100 grams of fresh tender corn instead of french beans and carrots.

Valval

Cooking time : 17 mins. 52 secs.   Serves 4

50 grams white pumpkin (lauki)
50 grams red pumpkin (kaddu)
50 grams ridge gourd (torai)
50 grams green peas
6 to 7 french beans
1 carrot
1/2 large fresh coconut
2 to 3 slit green chillies
2 to 3 curry leaves
1/2 tsp cumin seeds
1/2 tbsp plain flour (maida)
1/2 tsp ghee
1/2 tbsp sugar
salt to taste

1. Slice the pumpkins, ridge gourd, french beans and carrot very thinly.
2. Scrape the coconut. Add 1 1/2 teacups of water and blend in a liquidiser. Strain and take out all the milk.
3. Mix the coconut milk and the plain flour very well.
4. Put the ghee in a glass bowl and microwave on HIGH for about 10 to 12 seconds. Add the cumin seeds and fry for 5 to 6 seconds by microwaving on HIGH. Add the chillies and curry leaves and fry them by microwaving on HIGH for about 9 to 10 seconds.
5. Add the vegetables, 1/2 teacup of water, sugar and salt and microwave on HIGH for about 7 to 8 minutes.
6. When the vegetables are soft, add the coconut milk-flour mixture and microwave on HIGH for 3 to 3 1/2 minutes, stirring once in-between after 1 1/2 minutes.

* Serve hot.

Eggplant in Tomato Sauce

Cooking time : 16 mins. 24 secs.

2 medium eggplants (long variety)
1 to 2 tsp oil
salt to taste

For the tomato sauce

3/4 kg red tomatoes
3 cloves crushed garlic
2 onions
1/2 tsp chilli powder
1 tsp oregano or 1/4 tsp ajwain
(optional)
1 tsp sugar
salt to taste

1. Slice the eggplants.
2. Put the oil in a shallow dish and microwave on HIGH for about 12 seconds.
3. Spread the eggplant slices over the hot oil and sprinkle a little salt on top. Cover and microwave on HIGH for about 6 to 7 minutes.

For the tomato sauce

1. Chop the tomatoes and onions
2. Mix the tomatoes, onions and garlic in a glass bowl Cover and microwave on HIGH for 5 to 6 minutes.
3. Blend the mixture in a liquidiser.
4. Add the chilli powder, oregano, sugar and salt and microwave on HIGH for about 3 minutes.
5. Pour the prepared tomato sauce over the eggplant slices.
6. Cover the serving dish and microwave on HIGH for 10-12 seconds.

* Serve hot.

Vegetable Florentine

Cooking time : 13 mins. 12 secs.   **Serves 4**

For the spinach

3 teacups chopped spinach
1/2 onion, chopped
1 tsp plain flour (maida)
(optional)
1 green chilli, chopped
1 tbsp fresh cream
1/2 tbsp butter
salt and pepper to taste

For the vegetables

1 1/2 teacups chopped mixed
vegetables (french beans, carrots,
green peas)
1 1/2 teacups white sauce,
(see page 9)
1/2 teacup thick curds (optional)

For the topping

1 tbsp grated cooking cheese
salt and pepper to taste

For the spinach

1. Thoroughly wash the spinach and
   remove the thick stems.
2. Put the spinach in a plate and
   microwave on HIGH for 30
   seconds.
3. Blend the spinach to a smooth
   puree in a blender.
4. Put the butter in a glass bowl and
   microwave on HIGH for about 12
   seconds. Add the onion, flour and
   green chillies and microwave on
   HIGH for 1¹/₂ minutes.
5. Add the spinach, cream, salt and
   pepper and microwave on HIGH
   for 2 minutes.

For the vegetables

1. Put all the vegetables in a shallow
   dish and sprinkle 3 to 4
   tablespoons of water. Microwave
   on HIGH for about 5 to 6 minutes.
2. Mix the boiled vegetables with the
   remaining ingredients.

How to proceed

1. Spread the vegetables in the bowl
   containing the spinach mixture.
   Sprinkle the cheese on top and
   microwave on HIGH for 2 minutes.

* Serve hot.

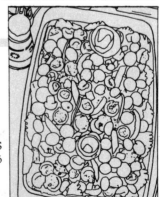

STUFFED MUSHROOMS
For recipe see page 36

Baked Stuffed Potatoes

Cooking time : 16 mins. 40 secs.

Serves 4

6 medium potatoes (old) with skin
3/4 teacup chopped mixed vegetables
(carrots, french beans, green peas)
1/2 onion, chopped
1/2 tsp chilli powder
1/2 tsp soya sauce
1 1/2 teacups white sauce,
(see page 9)
1/2 teacup thick curds
3 tbsp grated cooking cheese
a little butter
1 tbsp oil
salt and pepper to taste

1. Place the chopped vegetables in a shallow dish. Sprinkle 2 to 3 tablespoons of water and microwave on HIGH for about 3 to 4 minutes.
2. Cut each potato into 2 halves and microwave on HIGH for about 6 to 8 minutes or until baked.
3. Remove the skin and scoop out the centers.
4. Put the oil in a glass bowl and microwave on high for 10 seconds. Add the onions and microwave on HIGH for about 1 minute, stirring once in-between after 30 seconds.
5. Add the vegetables, scooped portion of the potatoes, chilli powder, soya sauce and salt and microwave on HIGH for about 1 minute, stirring once in-between after 30 seconds.
6. Fill the potato centers with the stuffing.
7. Add the curds, salt, pepper and half of the cheese to the white sauce.
8. Arrange the potatoes in a shallow dish, cover with the seasoned white sauce and the remaining cheese.
9. Dot with butter and microwave on HIGH for about 1½ minute.

* Serve immediately.

KHANDVI
For recipe see page 40

Baked Paneer in
Spinach with Tomato Sauce

Cooking time : 18 mins. 30 secs.   Serves 6

For the spinach

6 teacups chopped spinach
1 onion, chopped
2 tsp plain flour (maida)
3 green chillies, chopped
2 tsp oil
salt to taste

For the tomato sauce

1 teacup
(see page 8)

Other ingredients

200 gms. paneer, sliced
2 teacups chopped mixed vegetables
(French beans, carrots, cauliflower)

For the Spinach

1. Thoroughly wash the spinach and
   remove the thick stems.
2. Put the spinach in a glass bowl and
   microwave on HIGH for 30 seconds
   or until well cooked.
3. Blend in a liquidiser.
4. Put the oil in a glass bowl and
   microwave on HIGH for about 15
   seconds.
5. Add the onion and microwave on
   HIGH for about 1 minute, stirring
   once in-between after 30 seconds.
6. Add the flour and microwave on
   HIGH for 15 seconds.
7. Add the green chillies, spinach
   puree and salt and microwave on
   HIGH for 1 minute.

How to proceed

1. Put the vegetables in a shallow
   dish, sprinkle 5 to 6 tablespoons
   of water and microwave on HIGH
   for about 3 minutes.
2. Mix the spinach with the paneer,
   vegetables and salt and spread in
   a shallow dish.
3. Pour the tomato sauce on top. If
   you like, grate a little of the paneer
   and sprinkle on top.
4. Microwave on HIGH for 3 to 3¹/₂
   minutes.

* Serve immediately.

Vegetable Imperial

Cooking time : 11 mins.

1/2 teacup boiled spaghetti
1 small potato, cut lengthwise (like chips)
1 carrot, cut into long strips
50 grams cauliflower, cut into strips
1 small capsicum, cut into strips
a few asparagus pieces
a few mushroom pieces
2 teacups white sauce,
(see page 9)
3 tbsp fresh cream (optional)
50 grams cooking cheese
2 tbsp cheese biscuits (e.g. cheeselings)
2 tbsp bread crumbs
a little butter
salt and pepper to taste

1. Put the potato, carrot and cauliflower in a shallow dish. Sprinkle 3 to 4 tablespoons of water and microwave on HIGH for about 5 to 6 minutes.
2. Mix the white sauce and cream. Add salt and pepper and half the cheese.
3. Add the boiled vegetables, capsicum, asparagus, mushrooms and spaghetti. Mix well.
4. Crush the cheese biscuits and sprinkle on top.
5. Sprinkle the bread crumbs and the remaining cheese. Dot with butter and microwave on HIGH for 3 to 4 minutes.

* Serve immediately.

Mixed Dal

Cooking time : 19 mins. 20 secs.   Serves 4

1 tbsp moong dal
1 tbsp masoor dal
1 tbsp urad dal
1/2 tsp turmeric powder
1/2 tsp cumin seeds
2 tomatoes, chopped
1 onion, chopped
1 tsp chopped green chillies
1 tsp chopped ginger
1/2 tsp chilli powder
2 tbsp chopped coriander
2 tbsp butter
salt to taste

1. Put all the dals together in 2 teacups of pre-heated water in a big glass bowl and allow to soak for 30 minutes.
2. Add salt and turmeric powder. Cover and microwave on HIGH for 15 minutes or until cooked.
3. Put the butter in another glass bowl and microwave on HIGH for about 20 seconds. Add the cumin seeds and fry for 30 seconds by microwaving on HIGH.
4. Add the tomatoes, onion, green chillies, ginger, chilli powder, coriander, cooked dals and salt and microwave on HIGH for 3 minutes.

* Serve hot.

Western Dishes

Noodles with Tomato and Cheese Sauce

Cooking time : 22 mins.   Serves 4

For the noodles
250 grams boiled ribbon noodles
(see page 9)

For the tomato sauce

3/4 kg tomatoes
1 medium onion, finely chopped
1 medium carrot, finely chopped
1 stick celery, finely chopped
1 1/2 tbsp fresh cream
1/2 tsp chilli powder
1/2 tsp oregano
or a pinch of ajwain (optional)
1 to 2 tsp sugar
1 tbsp oil
1 tbsp grated cheese
salt to taste

For the cheese sauce

1 teacup cheese sauce
(see page 7)

For the tomato sauce
1. Put the tomatoes in a glass bowl
   and microwave on HIGH for 3
   to 4 minutes or until the skin is
   loosened.
2. Remove the skin and grate into a
   pulp. Add 1/2 teacup of water.
3. Put the oil in a glass bowl and
   microwave on HIGH for about 12
   seconds. Add the onion, carrot and
   celery and microwave on HIGH for
   40 to 45 seconds.
4. Add the tomato pulp, chilli
   powder, oregano, sugar and salt
   and microwave on HIGH for 10
   minutes, stirring once in-between
   after 5 minutes.
5. Add the cream and mix very well.

How to proceed
Put the noodles and the two sauces
and grated cheese in individual
serving dishes/bowls and let the
guests help themselves to the noodles
with desired toppings.

Macaroni Hot Pot

Cooking time : 19 mins. 30 secs.

Serves 4

3/4 teacup cooked shell macaroni, (see page 8)
1 1/2 onions
1 capsicum
3 large tomatoes
2 cloves garlic, crushed
1/2 tsp chilli powder
1 small can (225 grams) baked beans
5 to 6 tbsp tomato ketchup
50 grams grated cooking cheese
1 tbsp butter
salt to taste

1. Cut the onions and capsicums into rings
2. Put the tomatoes in a bowl and microwave on HIGH for about 3 to 4 minutes. Cool and remove the skins. Grate.
3. Put the butter in a glass bowl and microwave on HIGH for 12 seconds Add the onion rings and microwave on HIGH for 30 seconds.
4. Add the capsicum rings and microwave on HIGH for about 2 minutes.
5. Take out a few rings of onions and capsicum for decoration.
6. Add the garlic, tomato pulp and chilli ·powder and microwave on HIGH for 2 minutes, stirring once in-between after 1 minute.
7. Add the macaroni, beans, tomato ketchup and salt and mix very well.
8. Cover with the capsicum and onion rings and sprinkle the cheese on top.
9. Microwave on HIGH for about 3 to 3 1/2 minutes.

* Serve hot.

Macaroni Supreme

Cooking time : 10 mins. 50 secs.

2 teacups boiled macaroni,
(see page 9)
2 1/2 teacups white sauce,
(see page 9)
4 tbsp chopped parsley
a pinch of nutmeg powder
a pinch of dried or fresh oregano
3/4 teacup grated cooking cheese
1 medium tomato, sliced
a little butter
salt and pepper to taste

1. Add the parsley, nutmeg powder, oregano, salt and pepper and three-quarters of the cheese to the white sauce.
2. Add the macaroni and mix. Spread on a greased shallow dish and arrange tomato slices on top. Cover with the remaining cheese and dot with butter.
3. Microwave on HIGH for about 2½ minutes.

* Serve immediately.

Stuffed Mushrooms

PICTURE ON PAGE 27

Cooking time : 7 mins. 52 secs.

Makes 20 pieces

20 fresh large mushrooms
2 tsp butter

For the stuffing

1 teacup finely chopped parsley
2 slices fresh bread
1 onion, chopped
a few drops lemon juice

1/4tsp green chilli,chopped

2 tbsp butter
salt to taste

For the mushroom

Detach and discard the stems from the mushrooms. Wash the mushroom caps.

For the stuffing

1. Put the butter in a glass bowl and microwave on HIGH for about 20 seconds. Add the onion and microwave on HIGH for 1 minute, stirring once in-between after 30 seconds.
2. Add the green chilli and microwave on HIGH for about 20 seconds.
3. Crumble the bread slices.
4. Add the crumbled bread, parsley, lemon juice and salt. Mix well and microwave on HIGH for about 2 minutes, stirring once in-between after 1 minute.

How to proceed

1. Stuff the cavities of the mushroom caps with the stuffing.
2. Put the butter in a shallow glass dish and microwave on HIGH for about 12 seconds.
3. Arrange the stuffed mushrooms in the dish and sprinkle 1 tablespoon of water on top. Cover and microwave on HIGH for about 3 to 4 minutes.

* Serve hot.

Vegetable Polynesian Style

Cooking time : 9 mins. 40 secs.   **Serves 4**

1 fresh drinking coconut
250 grams mixed chopped vegetables
(carrots, french beans,
green peas, etc.)
1 tbsp cornflour
1/2 tsp cumin seeds
1 tbsp oil
salt to taste

To be ground into a paste

3 green chillies
1 medium onion
25 mm piece ginger

1. Take out the coconut water, scoop out the meat and blend both in a liquidiser with the cornflour.
2. Place the chopped vegetables in a shallow dish. Sprinkle 5 to 6 tablespoons of water on top and microwave on HIGH for about 3 to 4 minutes.
3. Put the oil in the bowl and microwave on HIGH for about 20 seconds. Add the cumin seeds and fry for 20 seconds by microwaving on HIGH. Add the paste and microwave on HIGH for 30 seconds.
4. Add the coconut milk mixture and microwave on HIGH for about 2 1/2 minutes, stirring in-between after every 30 seconds.
5. Add the vegetables and salt and microwave on HIGH for 2 minutes, stirring once in-between after 1 minute.
6. Fill the hot vegetable in the coconut shell.

* Serve immediately.

Spaghetti in Tomato Sauce

Cooking time : 4 mins. 50 secs.   Serves 6

2 teacups boiled spaghetti
(see page 9)
2 onions, chopped
1 capsicum (optional), cut into rings
2 teacup tomato sauce
(see page 8)
4 tbsp tomato ketchup
2 tbsp butter
100 grams fresh cream
100 grams grated cooking cheese
salt to taste

1. Put the butter in a bowl and microwave on HIGH for about 20 seconds. Add the onions and capsicum and microwave on HIGH for 1 minute. Keep aside a few capsicum rings for decoration.
2. Add the tomato sauce and salt and microwave on HIGH for about 2 minutes, stirring once in-between after 1 minute.
3. Add the tomato ketchup, spaghetti and cream and microwave on HIGH for about 1 1/2 minutes, stirring once in-between after 45 seconds.
4. Cover with the balance capsicum rings and the grated cheese.

* Serve hot.

Sweet and Sour Vegetable Stew

Cooking time : 13 mins. 35 secs.

Serves 6

175 grams french beans, cut into big pieces
175 grams carrots, cut into big pieces
175 grams cauliflower, cut into big pieces
175 gram potatoes, cut into big pieces
175 grams green peas
175 grams small onions
2 large onions, sliced
1 tomato, cut into big pieces
1 apple, cut into big pieces
1 small can (450 grams) pineapple slices, cut into big pieces
1 tbsp cornflour
3 cloves
2 sticks cinnamon
1/2 teacup tomato ketchup
1 tsp chilli powder
3 tbsp ghee
salt to taste

1. Place the french beans, carrots, cauliflower, potatoes, green peas and small onions in a shallow dish and sprinkle 7 to 8 tablespoons of water on top. Microwave on HIGH for about 7 to 8 minutes.
2. Mix the syrup from the pineapple can with the cornflour and keep aside.
3. Put the ghee in a glass bowl and microwave on HIGH for about 35 seconds. Add the sliced onions and microwave on HIGH for 2 minutes or until light pink in colour.
4. Add the cloves and cinnamon and microwave on HIGH for about 30 seconds.
5. Add the cooked vegetables and small onions and microwave on HIGH for about 30 seconds.
6. Add the tomato, apple and pineapple pieces, cornflour syrup, tomato ketchup, chilli powder and salt and microwave on HIGH for about 2 minutes, stirring once in-between after 1 minute.

* Serve hot.

Khandvi

PICTURE ON PAGE 28

Cooking time : 4 mins. 30 secs.   Serves 2

For khandvi

1/2 teacup gram flour (besan)
1/2 teacup curds mixed with 1/2 teacup water
(alternatively 1 teacup buttermilk)
1/2 tsp chilli-ginger paste
2 pinches turmeric powder
a pinch asafoetida
salt to taste

Other ingredients

3 tbsp grated coconut
2 tbsp chopped coriander

For the seasoning

2 tbsp oil
1 tsp mustard seeds
a pinch of asafoetida

For khandvi

1. Mix the flour, curd mixture, chilli-ginger paste, turmeric powder, asafoetida and salt very well in a large bowl.
2. Microwave on HIGH for 4-4½ minutes, stirring in-between after every 1½ minute.
3. Spread the mixture on a smooth kitchen platform or surface. Allow to cool for 2 to 3 minutes.
4. Slit the khandvi lengthwise every 40 mm along the width.
5. Carefully roll out each strip.

For the seasoning

Heat the oil on a flame. When hot, remove from the flame and add the mustard seeds and asafoetida.

How to proceed

1. Sprinkle the seasoning on top.
2. Decorate with the coconut and coriander.

* Serve hot.

Potato Rosti

PICTURE ON PAGE : 45

Cooking time : 20 mins. 12 secs.   **Serves 4**

500 grams potatoes (with jackets)
75 grams grated cheese
(use a combination of two cheeses)
1/2 onion, finely chopped
1 small green chilli, finely chopped
(optional)
1 tbsp butter
salt and pepper to taste

1. Wash the potatoes retaining the jackets.
2. Microwave on HIGH for about 5 to 6 minutes. the potatoes should be undercooked and remain firm.
3. Cool. Peel the potatoes and grate coarsely or slice. Sprinkle salt and pepper on top.
4. Put the butter in a glass bowl and microwave on HIGH for about 10 to 12 seconds.
5. Add the onion and microwave on HIGH for 2 minutes, stirring once in-between after 1 minute.
6. Add the potatoes, sprinkle the chilli and cheese on top and microwave on HIGH for 5 to 6 minutes.
7. Turn potato mixture upside down in one piece and again microwave on HIGH for 5 to 6 minutes.
8. Loosen around the edges with a knife, invert and take out in one piece.

* Serve hot.

Rice Dishes

Green Peas Pullav

Cooking time : 16 mins. 15 secs.   **Serves 2**

1 teacup uncooked Basmati rice
1 teacup green peas
2 sticks cinnamon
2 cloves
1 bay leaf
1 1/2 green chillies, chopped
4 tbsp chopped onion
2 tbsp ghee
salt to taste

1. Put the ghee in a glass bowl and microwave on HIGH for 15 seconds.
2. Add the cinnamon, cloves, bay leaf, green chillies and chopped onion. Microwave on HIGH for about 2 minutes, stirring once in-between after 1 minute.
3. Add the rice, green peas, 2 1/4 teacups of water and salt. Cover and microwave on HIGH for about 12-14 minutes, stirring once in-between after 5 to 6 minutes.

* Serve hot.

Masala Bhaat

Cooking time : 18 mins.

1/2 teacup uncooked Basmati rice
50 grams green peas
50 grams potatoes
50 grams brinjals
1 onion, chopped
2 tbsp chopped coriander
1/4 tsp turmeric powder
2 tsp coriander-cumin seed
(dhana-jira) powder
2 tsp chilli powder
3/4 tsp garam masala
1 1/2 tbsp ghee
salt to taste
1 tbsp chopped coriander for
decoration
To be ground into a paste
2 tbsp grated fresh coconut
2 green chillies
12 mm. piece ginger
5 to 6 cloves garlic

1. Cut the potatoes and brinjals into big pieces.
2. Mix the rice, vegetables, onion, coriander, turmeric powder, coriander-cumin seed powder, chilli powder, garam masala, paste, salt and ghee and add 1 1/2 teacups of water.
3. Cover and microwave on HIGH for 17 to 18 minutes, stirring in-between after every 5 to 6 minutes.
4. Decorate with chopped coriander.

* Serve hot.

Green Pullav

PICTURE ON PAGE : 46

Cooking time : 19 mins.   Serves 4

1 teacup uncooked Basmati rice
275 grams cauliflower, cut into big pieces
175 grams green peas
225 grams small potatoes (whole)
2 sticks cinnamon
2 cloves
2 cardamoms
2 bay leaves
2 onion chopped
4 tbsp ghee
salt to taste

To be ground into a paste

1 big bunch fresh coriander
6 green chillies
25 mm. piece ginger
10 cloves garlic

1. Put the ghee in a glass bowl and microwave on HIGH for about 30 seconds .
2. Add the onion and microwave on HIGH for 1½ minutes, stirring once in-between after 30 seconds.
3. Add the paste and microwave on HIGH for 1 minute, stirring once in-between after 30 seconds.
4. Add the cinnamon, cloves, cardamom and bay leaves and microwave on HIGH for 1 minute.
5. Add the rice, vegetables, salt and 2 teacups of water.
6. Cover and microwave on HIGH for about 15 minutes or until the water is absorbed and the vegetables are cooked.

* Serve with kadhi or curds.

POTATO ROSTI
For recipe see page 41

Curried Beans with Buttered Rice

Cooking time : 20 mins. 50 secs.   Serves 4

For the beans

1 large can (450 grams) baked beans
3 onions, finely chopped
3 cloves garlic crushed
1 tsp curry powder
1/2 tsp chilli powder
1/2 teacup tomato ketchup
2 tbsp butter
salt to taste

For the buttered rice

1 1/2 teacups uncooked Basmati rice
2 tbsp butter
salt to taste

For the beans

1. Put the butter in a glass bowl and microwave on HIGH for about 20 seconds .
2. Add the onions, crushed garlic and microwave on HIGH for about 1 minute, stirring once in-between after 30 seconds.
3. Add the curry powder and chilli powder and microwave on HIGH for 30 seconds.
4. Add the baked beans, tomato ketchup and salt and microwave on HIGH for 2 1/2 to 3 minutes stirring in-between after every 30 seconds.

* Serve hot with buttered rice.

For the buttered rice

1. Put the rice and salt in a glass bowl add 3 teacups of water.
2. Microwave on HIGH for about 14 to 15 minutes or until cooked, stirring in-between after about 7 minutes. Each grain of the cooked rice should be separate.
3. Put the butter in another glass bowl and microwave on HIGH for about 30 seconds.
4. Add the cooked rice and mix well. Microwave on HIGH for about 30 seconds.

* Serve hot.

GREEN PULLAV
For recipe see page 44

47

Savoury Rice with Vegetables

Cooking time : 16 mins. 50 secs.   **Serves 4**

3/4 teacups uncooked rice
50 grams carrots, chopped
50 grams green peas
1 potato, chopped
2 medium onions, sliced
150 grams cauliflower, chopped
juice of 1 lemon
2 tbsp ghee
salt to taste

For decoration
fried onion slices
fried cashewnuts

To be ground into a paste
1 tbsp grated fresh coconut
2 green chillies
4 cloves
2 to 3 cardamoms
2 small stick cinnamon
1 tsp khus-khus
12 mm. piece ginger

1. Put the ghee in a glass bowl and microwave on HIGH for about 30 seconds. Add the onions and microwave on HIGH for 1 minute or until light pink in colour.
2. Add the paste and microwave on HIGH for 20 seconds.
3. Add the rice, vegetables, lemon juice and salt and mix very well. Add 1 3/4 teacups of water and microwave on HIGH for 12 minutes, stirring in-between after every 3 minutes.
4. Put off the cooker and allow to stand for 3 minutes.
5. Decorate with fried onions and cashewnuts.

* Serve hot.

Moongdal Khichadi

Cooking time : 15 mins. 30 secs.   **Serves 4**

1 teacup uncooked rice
1 teacup sprouted moong
2 to 3 pinches asafoetida
1/4 tsp turmeric powder
2 tbsp ghee
To be mixed together in masala mixture
2 tsp coriander-cumin seed (dhana-jira) powder
2 tsp sugar
1 tsp chilli powder
2 tbsp grated fresh coconut
2 tbsp chopped coriander
a pinch asafoetida
salt to taste

1. Wash the rice. Drain.
2. Wash the moong sprouts. Drain.
3. Put the ghee in a glass bowl and microwave on HIGH for about 30 seconds.
4. Add the rice, moong sprouts, asafoetida, turmeric powder, masala mixture and 2 1/2 teacups of water.
5. Cover and microwave on HIGH for about 15 minutes, stirring in-between after every 5 minutes.

* Serve hot.

Desserts

Quick Bread and Butter Pudding with Tangy Sauce

Cooking time : 4 mins.   **Serves 2**

2 large fresh bread slices
2 teacups milk
10 tsp sugar
5 to 6 drops vanilla essence
4 tsp butter

For the sauce

4 tbsp marmalade
5 to 6 drops lemon juice

For the pudding

1. Grease a shallow dish with 1 teaspoon of butter.
2. Mix the milk, sugar and essence.
3. Place the bread slices in the dish, pour the sweetened milk on top and dot with the remaining butter. Microwave on HIGH for 4 minutes.

For the sauce

Dissolve the marmalade in the lemon juice.

How to serve

Pour the sauce over the bread slice and serve.

Banana Flambe'

4 bananas
50 grams brown sugar
1 tbsp butter
3 tbsp brandy
sweetened cream or
 vanilla ice-cream to serve

1. Cut the bananas lengthwise and place in a pan with the cut side down.
2. Add the sugar, butter and microwave on HIGH for 2 to 3 minutes, turning the bananas 3 to 4 times in-between to prevent them from becoming soggy.
3. Just before serving, pour the brandy into a large spoon and warm on a flame. Set alight and pour the burning brandy over the bananas.

* Serve at once with sweetened cream or with vanilla ice-cream.

Pineapple Flambe'

Cooking time : 4 mins. 42 secs.   Serves 6

6 pineapple slices (from can)
2 tbsp honey
2 tbsp orange juice
2 tbsp brandy
6 cherries (from can)
1 tbsp butter
whipped cream or
vanilla ice-cream to serve

1. Put the butter in a shallow dish and microwave on HIGH for about 12 seconds.
2. Arrange the pineapple slices in the dish, put one cherry in center of each slice and microwave on HIGH for 2 to 3 minutes.
3. Add the honey and orange juice and microwave on HIGH for 1 1/2 minutes.
4. Just before serving, pour the brandy into a large spoon and warm on a flame. Set alight and pour the burning brandy over the fruit.

* Serve with whipped cream or with vanilla ice-cream as desired.

Apple Crumble

Cooking time : 12 mins.   **Serves 4**

1 teacup plain flour (maida)
a pinch salt
6 tbsp butter
100 grams granulated or brown sugar
700 grams cooking apples, peeled and
sliced
2 to 3 pinches ground cinnamon

1. Sieve the flour and salt together into a mixing bowl and rub in the butter until the mixture resembles fine bread crumbs.
2. Add 40 grams of sugar and mix very well.
3. Spread the apple slices evenly in a shallow dish, add 50 grams of sugar and ground cinnamon.
4. Cover and microwave on HIGH for 3 to 4 minutes.
5. Top with the crumbled flour mixture, press very well, and sprinkle with the remaining sugar and a pinch of ground cinnamon. Microwave on HIGH for 6 to 8 minutes or until just set.

* Serve immediately.

Fresh Peach Stew

Cooking time : 8 mins.   **Serves 4**

6 fresh peaches
4 tbsp sugar
2 sticks cinnamon
1 tsp lemon juice
2 cloves

1. Cut the peaches into halves, peel and remove the stones.
2. Put the sugar, lemon juice, cinnamon, cloves and 3/4 teacup of water in a bowl.
3. Add the peach pieces and microwave on HIGH for about 6 to 8 minutes or until soft.
4. Chill.

* Serve cold.

Fresh Apple Stew

Cooking time : 8 mins.   **Serves 4**

4 fresh apples, medium size
4 to 6 tbsp sugar
2 sticks cinnamon
1 tsp lemon juice
2 cloves

1. Divide the apples into halves. Peel and remove the seeds and keep in salted water to prevent browning.
2. Put the sugar, lemon juice, cinnamon, cloves and 3/4 teacup of water in a bowl.
3. Add the apple pieces and microwave on HIGH for about 6 to 8 minutes or until soft.
4. Chill.

* Serve cold.

CHOCOLATE FONDUE
For recipe see page 58

54

Apple and Raisin Pudding

Cooking time : 3 mins.   **Serves 6**

6 large dessert apples, peeled and
sliced
2 tbsp raisins
6 to 7 tablespoons brown sugar
1 tsp cinnamon powder
1 tsp lemon juice
2 to 3 tbsp rum or brandy(optional)
a little butter

1. Soak the raisins in 2 to 3
   tablespoons of rum (or water) for
   1 hour.
2. Arrange the apple slices in a
   shallow dish and add the soaked
   raisins with liquid.
3. Add the sugar, cinnamon powder
   and lemon juice and mix. Dot with
   a little butter.
4. Cover and microwave on HIGH for
   about 3 minutes.

* Serve immediately.

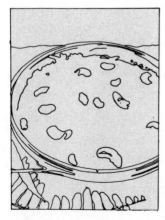

CARROT HALWA
For recipe see page 61

Chocolate Fondue

PICTURE ON PAGE : 55

Cooking time : 5 mins. 30 secs.

Serves 6

100 grams plain or milk chocolate, broken into small pieces
1 tbsp plain flour (maida)
1/2 teacup milk
3 tbsp cocoa (approx.)*
200 grams beaten cream
4 to 5 tbsp sugar
1/2 tsp vanilla essence
1 tbsp butter
2 tbsp brandy (optional)
stewed or fresh fruit, marshmallows, cake pieces for dipping

* Adjust the quantity of cocoa according to its strength.

1. Put the butter in a glass bowl and add the flour. Microwave on MEDIUM for $1^{1}/_{2}$ minutes, stirring twice in-between after every 30 seconds.

2. Add the milk, chocolate pieces, cocoa, cream, sugar and 1 teacup of water Microwave on MEDIUM for about 3 to 4 minutes or until mixture becomes thick, stirring in-between after every 30 seconds.

3. Put the mixture in a chafing dish. Stir in the vanilla essence and brandy.

* Let your guests serve themselves by dipping fruit, marshmallow or cake pieces in the hot mixture.

Cherry Jubilee

Cooking time : 4 mins.

Serves 8

1 small can (450 grams) cherries
1 1/2 tsp cornflour
2 tsp raspberry jam
2 tsp sugar
2 tsp lemon juice
a few drops cochineal
2 tbsp brandy
whipped cream or vanilla ice-cream
to serve

1. Stone the cherries. Keep aside the syrup.
2. To the cherry syrup, add the cornflour, jam and sugar and microwave on HIGH for about 3 to 4 minutes or until the mixture reaches pouring consistency, stirring in-between after every 30 seconds.
3. Add the lemon juice, cochineal and the cherries. Mix very well.
4. Just before serving, pouring the brandy into a large spoon and warm on a flame. Set alight and pour the burning brandy over the cherries. Mix well.

* Serve immediately with whipped cream or with vanilla ice-cream as desired.

Sooji Seera

Cooking time : 9 mins. 45 secs.   Serves 4

1/2 teacup semolina (sooji / rawa)
1/2 teacup milk
6 tbsp sugar
3 tbsp ghee
1/4 tsp cardamom powder

1. Put the milk, sugar and 1 1/2 teacups of water in a glass bowl and microwave on HIGH for about 5 minutes, stirring once in-between after 2 1/2 minutes. Keep aside.
2. Put the ghee in another glass bowl and microwave on HIGH for about 15 seconds.
3. Add the semolina, mix well and microwave on HIGH for 3 minutes, stirring in-between after every 1 minute or until the semolina is light pink in colour.
4. Add the preboiled sweetened milk mixture. Mix well and microwave on HIGH for 1 1/2 minutes, stirring in-between after every 30 seconds.
5. Sprinkle cardamom powder on top.

* Serve hot.

Carrot Halwa

PICTURE ON PAGE : 56

Cooking time : 10 mins. 45 secs.   **Serves 4**

2 teacups grated carrot
1/2 teacup milk
6 tbsp sugar
4 tbsp fresh khoya
2 tbsp ghee
a pinch cardamom powder
2 tbsp fresh cream

1. Put the ghee in a bowl and microwave on HIGH for about 15 seconds.
2. Add the carrot and stir well. Microwave on HIGH for about 2 minutes.
3. Mix the milk, sugar and khoya and add to the carrot. Microwave on HIGH for 7 to 8 minutes, stirring in-between after every 2 1/2 to 3 minutes.
4. Sprinkle the cardamom powder on top, dot with the fresh cream and microwave on HIGH for 30 seconds.

* Serve hot.

Almonds Rocks

Cooking time : 15 mins.

Makes 50 pieces

400 grams small almonds, coarsely
sliced
400 grams plain chocolate
100 grams milk chocolate

1. Spread the almond slices evenly
   in a plate and microwave on HIGH
   for about 5 to 7 minutes or until
   light pink in colour. Stir
   in-between after every 30 seconds
   to obtain even colour. Cool.
2. Break up the chocolate into small
   pieces and put into small bowl.
   Microwave on LOW for about 8
   minutes, stirring once in- between
   after 4 minutes. The chocolate will
   first become shiny and then begin
   to lose its shape. Continue
   microwaving for a little longer
   period until it melts, stirring
   in-between after every 1 minute.
   Do not overcook as otherwise the
   chocolate will burn.
3. Remove from the oven and
   continually stir the chocolate until
   it cools a little. Add the almond
   pieces and mix well.
4. Put small pieces of the coated
   almonds on a tray lined with
   grease-proof paper or with
   aluminium foil. Keep in the
   refrigerator for 2 hours.
5. Wrap in decorative foil and store
   in refrigerator.